Sutherland

by Colin Sutherland

LangSyne
PUBLISHING
WRITING *to* REMEMBER

Lang**Syne**

PUBLISHING

WRITING *to* REMEMBER

79 Main Street, Newtongrange,
Midlothian EH22 4NA
Tel: 0131 344 0414   Fax: 0845 075 6085
E-mail: info@lang-syne.co.uk
www.langsyneshop.co.uk

Design by Dorothy Meikle
Printed by Ricoh Print Scotland
© Lang Syne Publishers Ltd 2015

ISBN 978-1-85217-085-1

Sutherland

SEPT NAMES INCLUDE:

Cheyne
Clyne
Duffy
Gray
Keith
Mowatt
Murray
Oliphant

Sutherland

MOTTO:
Without Fear

CREST:
A wildcat sitting erect

TERRITORY:
Caithness and Sutherland

Chapter one:

The origins of the clan system

by Rennie McOwan

The original Scottish clans of the Highlands and the great families of the Lowlands and Borders were gatherings of families, relatives, allies and neighbours for mutual protection against rivals or invaders.

Scotland experienced invasion from the Vikings, the Romans and English armies from the south. The Norman invasion of what is now England also had an influence on land-holding in Scotland. Some of these invaders stayed on and in time became 'Scottish'.

The word clan derives from the Gaelic language term 'clann', meaning children, and it was first used many centuries ago as communities were formed around tribal lands in glens and mountain fastnesses.

The format of clans changed over the centuries, but at its best the chief and his family held the land on behalf of all, like trustees, and the ordinary clansmen and women believed they had a blood relationship with the founder of their clan.

There were two way duties and obligations. An inadequate chief could be deposed and replaced by someone of greater ability.

Clan people had an immense pride in race. Their relationship with the chief was like adult children to a father and they had a real dignity.

The concept of clanship is very old and a more feudal notion of authority gradually crept in.

Pictland, for instance, was divided into seven principalities ruled by feudal leaders who were the strongest and most charismatic leaders of their particular groups.

By the sixth century the 'British' kingdoms of Strathclyde, Lothian and Celtic Dalriada (Argyll) had emerged and Scotland, as one nation, began to take shape in the time of King Kenneth MacAlpin.

Some chiefs claimed descent from

ancient kings which may not have been accurate in every case.

By the twelfth and thirteenth centuries the clans and families were more strongly brought under the central control of Scottish monarchs.

Lands were awarded and administered more and more under royal favour, yet the power of the area clan chiefs was still very great.

The long wars to ensure Scotland's independence against the expansionist ideas of English monarchs extended the influence of some clans and reduced the lands of others.

Those who supported Scotland's greatest king, Robert the Bruce, were awarded the territories of the families who had opposed his claim to the Scottish throne.

In the Scottish Borders country – the notorious Debatable Lands – the great families built up a ferocious reputation for providing warlike men accustomed to raiding into England and occasionally fighting one another.

Chiefs had the power to dispense justice and to confiscate lands and clan warfare produced a society where martial virtues – courage, hardiness, tenacity – were greatly admired.

Gradually the relationship between the clans and the Crown became strained as Scottish monarchs became more orientated to life in the Lowlands and, on occasion, towards England.

The Highland clans spoke a different language, Gaelic, whereas the language of Lowland Scotland and the court was Scots and in more modern times, English.

Highlanders dressed differently, had different customs, and their wild mountain land sometimes seemed almost foreign to people living in the Lowlands.

It must be emphasised that Gaelic culture was very rich and story-telling, poetry, piping, the clarsach (harp) and other music all flourished and were greatly respected.

Highland culture was different from other parts of Scotland but it was not inferior or less sophisticated.

Central Government, whether in London or Edinburgh, sometimes saw the Gaelic clans as

*"The spirit of the clan means much
to thousands of people"*

a challenge to their authority and some sent expeditions into the Highlands and west to crush the power of the Lords of the Isles.

Nevertheless, when the eighteenth century Jacobite Risings came along the cause of the Stuarts was mainly supported by Highland clans.

The word Jacobite comes from the Latin for James – Jacobus. The Jacobites wanted to restore the exiled Stuarts to the throne of Britain.

The monarchies of Scotland and England became one in 1603 when King James VI of Scotland (1st of England) gained the English throne after Queen Elizabeth died.

The Union of Parliaments of Scotland and England, the Treaty of Union, took place in 1707.

Some Highland clans, of course, and Lowland families opposed the Jacobites and supported the incoming Hanoverians.

After the Jacobite cause finally went down at Culloden in 1746 a kind of ethnic cleansing took place. The power of the chiefs was curtailed. Tartan and the pipes were banned in law.

Many emigrated, some because they

wanted to, some because they were evicted by force. In addition, many Highlanders left for the cities of the south to seek work.

Many of the clan lands became home to sheep and deer shooting estates.

But the warlike traditions of the clans and the great Lowland and Border families lived on, with their descendants fighting bravely for freedom in two world wars.

Remember the men from whence you came, says the Gaelic proverb, and to that could be added the role of many heroic women.

The spirit of the clan, of having roots, whether Highland or Lowland, means much to thousands of people.

A map of the clans' homelands

Chapter two:

Revenge and repression

The Sutherlands' history is overshadowed by the Clearances of 1814 to 1820 and the bitter controversy which followed them.

Until that date they were one of the best examples of co-operation between Gaelic clansmen and a non-Gaelic chieftain line.

But the Clearances in a mere decade brought about the most spectacular collapse of clan loyalty in Highland history. The Lairdship of Sutherland forms an instructive paradox – how did the most northerly part of mainland Scotland become known as the southland? Because to the Norsemen, who first conquered it, it was to the south, not only of their Norwegian homeland but to the south of their great Scottish provinces which in the 10th and 11th centuries included the whole of the modern counties of Caithness and Sutherland (which they called 'Sudderland').

The Sutherland family established itself by helping to drive them out. Their first known ancestor was a Flemish mercenary called Freskin who was given a commission by King David the First to gather all the Sutherland Gaels together to clear the Norsemen from the north. Freskin was therefore probably the hero of the first great clan legend – the story of the Killing of the Last Norsemen, the crucial battle which are told took place at Embol near Dornoch where the Norse chief had gathered all his men in a desperate attempt to reverse the Scottish advance. Indeed the fight at first went the Norsemens' way when they penetrated to the heart of the Scots' formation and cut the Sutherland chief to the ground. As the chief lay wounded, though, he spotted the

Norse General coming up to support the attack and, finding a horseshoe conveniently at hand, threw it with all his force, striking the Norseman square on the forehead and turning the whole battle round.

The Lordship of Sutherland title was first given to one, Hugo, who strengthened the family's royal favour by ridding the north of a ferocious robber band whose leader was called Chisholm. Among other crimes this Chisholm tortured a number of Sutherland churchmen by nailing horseshoes to their feet and making them dance to entertain his followers before putting them savagely to death. On hearing of this outrage, King William the Lion ordered Hugo of Sutherland to pursue Chisholm to the death and a great fight ensued near John O'Groats in which all the robbers were either killed or captured. Chisholm and the other leaders were given a punishment to fit the crime – horse-shoeing and hanging, the rest being castrated "less any succession should spring from so detestable a breed".

In 1222 trouble started with a row over

rights imposed by the Bishop of Caithness. His seat was at Dornoch and the Sinclair Earls of Caithness, based at Wick and Thurso, had long resented the fact that the bishopric was under Dornoch Sutherland control. Therefore, Caithness determined to exploit the discontent to get rid of the bishop and have the seat moved. Soon there was a riot incited by the Caithness supporters and the unfortunate Bishop was roasted alive on his own cow spit and soon the rioters were heading north. Once again the Lord of Sutherland was given responsibility by the Crown for restoring law and order and punishing Caithness for his instigation of the incident. The far north east was ravaged by a ferocious campaign of revenge and repression. Wick and Thurso were burned, the Caithness stronghold raised to the ground and 80 men beheaded or hanged in a summary court session at Golspie. To the end there was strict punishment for the rioters. Four of the ringleaders were roasted on their cow spit and then fed to the Crown dogs for good measure. This campaign set the pattern for the centuries to follow.

Chapter three:

The great slaughter

**By 1275 the earls of Sutherland had taken
Sutherland as their family name as well. Their
close allies were the Bishops of Caithness, the
Scottish Crown and the Gaelic clansmen
round Dornoch and Helmsdale. Their habitual
enemies were the Sinclairs of Caithness, the
MacKays from the far North West and the
MacLeods of Assynt.**

It was the backing of the Crown which
mattered most and this was retained by the
Sutherlands through their services during the War
of Independence, culminating in the success of the
5th Earl William who in 1343 married King
David Bruce's sister and who won many favours
from him, including the overlordship of the
MacKay lands of Strathnaver, the captaincy of
Dunnottar Castle south of Aberdeen and, lastly,
the very succession to the Scottish Crown itself
for his son by Margaret Bruce. Both the latter gifts

lapsed since the son died and Dunnottar was given up as too far from the Sutherland homeland but the expansion into Strathnaver was crucial since it was the first and largest step towards the Sutherlands' eventual ownership of almost all of the county which bears their name.

However, before that, in 1500 the Gordons took over the Earldom of Sutherland. The long dispute with the MacKays first came to a head in 1372 when the head of one of the junior branches, Nicholas Sutherland, treacherously murdered MacKay and his heir in their beds at Dingwall Castle for both sides had met in an attempt to patch up their quarrel. Much bloodshed followed these killings, including a retaliatory raid on Dornoch in which the much-wronged cathedral was once again set on fire and Sutherland men hanged in the town square.

After this the feud quietened down as both sides were called away to fight against the English. Robert Sutherland, the sixth Earl, stood with Douglas against Percy at the famous moon-light battle of Otterburn in 1388; and in the lull brought about by the English wars built the strong fortress of Dunrobin to secure himself and his men in future clan conflicts. His long chieftainship even saw a temporary alliance with the MacKays against the MacLeods who invaded Strathnavar in 1407 after rumours that MacKay was mistreating his wife, a MacLeod heiress. Since both Sutherland and MacKay country was laid waste, the old rivals joined forces to pursue the MacLeods as they returned east, catching them somewhere near Loch Shin where the invaders were massacred to the last man.

This day became known as the Great Slaughter and gave the Sutherlands the upper hand in Assynt, completing their domination of local clan rivals but there was one weakness running through the Sutherland history, always threatening to destroy them. Their line was ancient, although not in the legendary sense of many of the Gaelic families, and the rights to the title and estates were always open to challenge. There was no charter for the Earldom though it was widely recognised to be the oldest in Scotland and there were many obscurities in their descent. It was always possible for a cadet branch, or even a complete outsider, to claim superior descent from some half-forgotten ancestor and to successfully challenge the ruling line to show otherwise. This is what happened at the end of the 15th century when the male line was eliminated and the Gordons took over the Earldom.

The central figure in this change was John Sutherland, eighth Earl who in a long reign of 30 years from 1460 seemed to have secured his house by patching up the MacKay feud again and by eliminating contenders for his position like the two illegitimate brothers he stabbed while playing football in 1470. He made a fatal mistake, though, in marrying his daughter Elizabeth to Adam Gordon of Aboyne, younger son of the ambitious Earl of Huntly and a man whose family had a long standing claim to the Sutherland estate. In 1494 Gordon and his wife obtained a claim of idiocy against the Earl, who was kept in close confinement for the next 14 years. When he died, the same couple had his eldest son declared incapable, too, and the estates put into their effective control although officially both title and lands reverted to the Crown. After Flodden in 1513 when the King and a great many of the great nobles, except the earl of Huntly, were killed, Adam Gordon and his wife had a free hand and were soon styling themselves Earl and Countess of Sutherland.

There was another claimant, though – Alexander Sutherland, son of the old Earl by his second marriage. The Gordons dealt with this threat by having a writ of bastardy written against

Alexander and banishing him from Sutherland where the clansmen were dangerously inclined to his cause.

A couple of years later Alexander succeeded in raising a force against the new regime and in winning temporary control of Dornoch but his supporters fled when the Gordon army attacked them and Alexander was quickly captured and beheaded. His head soon perched on the loftiest point of the cathedral. This fulfilled the prophecy of a local witch who had told him that his head would be the highest that ever was in Sutherland, though doubtless Alexander himself had interpreted the saying rather differently.

Chapter four:

Poison and treason

**The Clan Sutherland was now part of the
Gordon empire of the North. Its chief
remained very conscious of the doubtful basis
of its tenure. In 1601 they obtained a new grant
of regality on vice-regal power from James the
Sixth which contained the extraordinary
provision that should their line fail the
Earldom and Estates would pass to another
Gordon house with no connection whatever to
the old Sutherland line.**

As a result, there was something of a
realignment of the north with the disinherited
Sutherland cadets allying themselves with the
old enemy of the Earldom, the Sinclairs and
MacKays; while the Earls turned to their Gordon
cousins in Moray and Buchan. The former party
had had its first chance to strike in 1562 when
Huntly, in rebellion against the Reformation, was
defeated by the Earl of Moray in Aberdeenshire

and the entire Gordon family, including the Earl of Sutherland, declared forfeit. The Earl of Caithness obtained a right of sequestration on the Sutherland estates and though the Gordons were restored by Queen Mary in 1566 there was virtual war all over the district for the next 30 years and the Sinclairs struggled yet again to get control of the great estates to their south.

Their greatest coup was the assassination of the Earl of Sutherland and his wife at Helmsdale Castle in 1567. This was arranged by Isobel Sinclair, the widow of a Sutherland cadet, who hoped to obtain the estates for her son when the Earl's family called at her castle after a day's hunting. She prepared a poisoned meal and served it in her private apartment so that she could watch its effect. Unfortunately for her, the Earl's heir, Alexander, had gone back out to continue the hunt. By the time he returned, the Earl and his wife had already began to feel the poison at work. Staggering to his feet, as his son came into the room the Earl gathered up the entire meal on the tablecloth and threw it from the window, saying,

"We are all poisoned here, Alex, let's back to Dunrobin where the Sinclair bitch can harm us no more!" The plot misfired when Isobel's own son, who had returned to the hunt with Alexander Gordon, went straight to the kitchen where unsuspecting servants gave him the remains of the poisoned food. He, the Earl and the Countess died in horrible agony two days later and Isobel was tried and condemned for the murder, cheating the hangman by committing suicide the night before her execution.

Chapter five:

The Clearances

Gordon and Murray were now the two commonest names. Sutherland was confined to the few pockets of clansmen immediately subject to the survivors of the old line. The land was wild and isolated, especially in winter when the weather invariably closed the few routes to the south.

On one occasion the Earl was caught in a blizzard between Dornoch and Dunrobin but wisely declined offers of cheering whisky, preferring a clear head to a warm throat. Sure enough, one after another, his piper, his chamberlain, his bodyguard and even his serving boy wandered off the track into the snow and were never seen again. The Earl alone reached his castle in safety with an understandable vow never to carry whisky in his train again which doubtless like most vows of its kind in the Highlands was kept only for a few months.

The clan began to acquire the reputation for enthusiastic Protestantism which distinguished its later history. This is probably what made the Earls begin to distance themselves from their Gordon cousins who were Catholics and later Jacobites.

In 1702 the break with Huntly became complete when the chief dropped the Gordon surname and reverted to the territorial title and soon Sutherlands were spreading again throughout the district as the clansmen in Gaelic fashion adopted their chief's patron image. There is evidence of this process at a Dornoch witch trial of 1722, the last such case in Scotland, where almost all the court officials were called Sutherland.

Various factors combined to make the '45 a complete disaster for the Sutherlanders, even though they were on the winning side. First, the Earl failed to raise and arm the clan quickly enough to take effective action against the Pretender when he was on the islands thus incurring suspicions of his loyalty in London. Then he was forced to disband the militia as the clansmen deserted to bring in the harvest, leaving Sutherland open to the rebels when they returned north in February, 1746. This led to the last storming of a fortress in British history when the Jacobite Earl of Cromarty brought 500 rebels against Dunrobin, narrowly missing its owner who was forced to flee by a back entrance and take ship for Aberdeen where he joined Cumberland's army. The Earl then spent the next four years in a vain attempt to obtain compensation for the extensive damage done to his estates by the rebels before dying, prematurely worn out by financial worries, in 1750.

In fact, the only redeeming episode of the '45 for the Sutherland men was the victory gained over the Earl of Cromarty's force as it retreated to join Prince Charlie at Culloden.

Unfortunately, the 19th century Sutherland family's estate managers were men of progressive, well-intentioned but unshakeably ruthless convictions who believed in the need to replace subsistence farming with a more rational system — sheep on the hills, the population on the coast and fishing and manufacturing. These 'improvements' proved drastic in scale and unfeeling, to say the least, in method. Clansmen were given notice to quit their mountain hovels and remove to specially prepared cottage plots on the coast. When they refused, managers simply burned their homes to the ground, sometimes over the owners' heads.

The tenants felt abandoned by those supposed to protect them. Their plight was made worse by the failure of the new industries and agriculture on the coast so that, when the second great clearance came in 1819, many preferred emigration to resettlement.

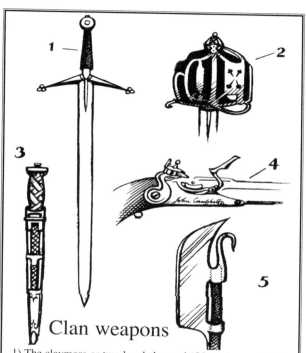

Clan weapons

1) The claymore or two-handed sword *(fifteenth or early six-teenth century)*
2) Basket hilt of broadsword made in Stirling, 1716
3) Highland dirk *(eighteenth century)*
4) Steel pistol *(detail)* made in Doune
5) Head of Lochaber Axe as carried in the '45 and earlier